Autumn
by the Sea

DEARESTFOLK POETRY

Cover Art by Adriaen Coorte, "Shells on a Stone Plinth"
1698, Netherlands

For permission requests, please contact:
hello@dearestfolkpoetry.com

ISBN: 979-8-9932201-0-9

DEDICATED TO THOSE WHO
FIND THEMSELVES AT SEA

and here you may find me
on almost any morning
walking along the shore

MARY OLIVER

Table of Contents

SEC. I

The Poetry of Sand

Autumn
by the
Sea

my feet did not know the way,
but my heart did—
heaving like waves in this cage of a chest
she silently beat straight to the coast
and collided into a strange shore,
churning my world like shipwrecked leftovers

teach my legs how to walk again—
i have been long lost at sea,
only knowing green—
but now my heart is changing color

Autumn by the *Sea*

the sand did its best to remain the same—
but everything changes once touched by the sea

keep me,
        summer ebbs—

    i will carry you as long as i can,
                        september says

Autumn
by the Sea

when it all begins to end
i find myself at sea
where i can lock eyes
with the endlessness—

i suffer from a delicate fear of looking,
        i told the sea,
            i'm wildly afraid of what i might find

the sea gave a knowing nod,
            if it's the deep you fear,
            you can always start at the shore

Autumn
by the Sea

i can be violent, too, autumn tells the tides,
and the waves believe—carrying her tales
to the ends of the earth like an old sailor
who hopes to warn all who might fall into
her arms

autumn learns from the low tide
that somehow being pulled apart
from all you know, *makes you grow*

Autumn by the Sea

the day the moths arrived i knew it was over—
and as delicately as it began, it unraveled all the same

THE MOON TRIED TO BRING
EVERYTHING BACK THAT WANED

Autumn *by the* Sea

maybe all the shells
are the spaces we carve
when we are stuck
somewhere between
knowing what's coming
and denying the ending

summer grew quieter
by a few dozen words
—even the stars began
to look paired away

Autumn
by the
Sea

my breath ran away today—
leaving me with nothing to breathe but sea

the way summer grew up and became autumn
breaks my heart each september

Autumn by the Sea

cattails swayed
with the same current
that caught me
—buoyed arms bobbing
in wild warning
to swim back to shore

the sea takes the mountain i hold
and moves it through autumn
until all that remains is a whisper of sand

Autumn
by the *Sea*

there are seasons in life when
two opposing feelings coincide—
sifting together like sand and stone
until one will rise, and the other, fall

some days
i am the sand—
but earth knows
i am doing my best

Autumn
by the Sea

it seems august and september both
listen to the sea but hear different things
and so i nestle myself against the tides
to make sense of their rushing advice—

hold on, let go
hold on, let go
hold on, let go

i cast my net of problems on the backs of waves
and wait in faith until i catch hope

Autumn
by the
Sea

the gulls dip beneath the september mist,
wings just barely breaking through the sea—
and i wonder if i, too, can stretch
myself between two worlds

my heart is a linen dress—
hem heavy with sea
a bronze monument frozen
that billows for release

Autumn
by the Sea

autumn tethered a rope to the leaves—
hoisted their sails into the wind
and promised them new lands

i bottled up the sand as a quiet promise
to remember how hard she tried to keep her castles

Autumn
by the Sea

MAYBE SAND IS THE DUST

OF EVERY FALLEN STAR

we cannot go back,
september replied—
but we will walk together until our hearts align

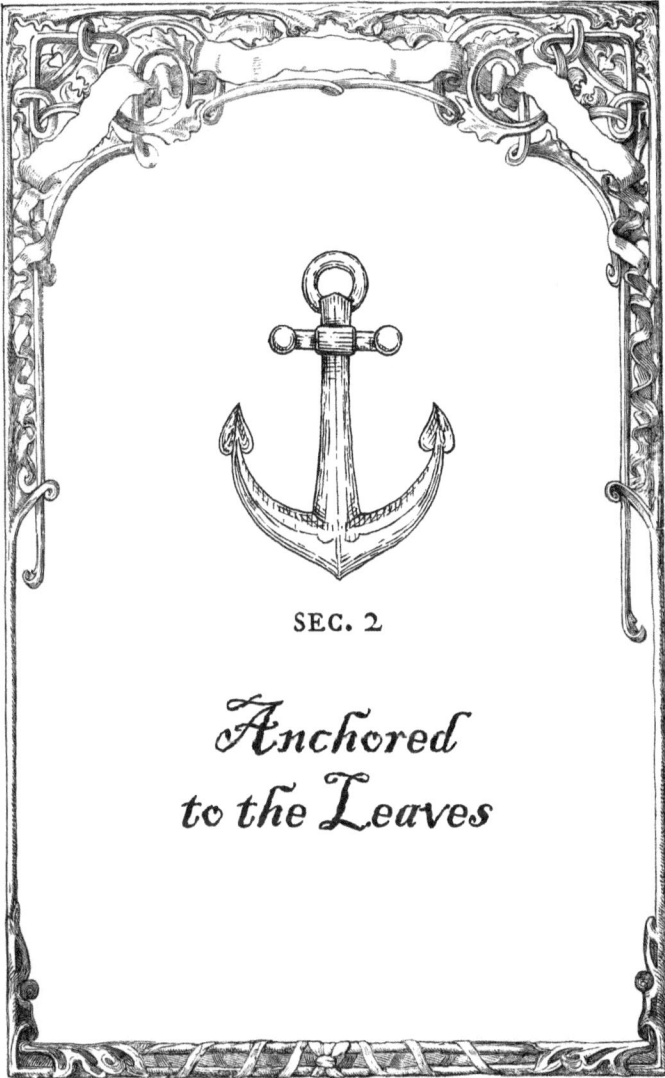

SEC. 2

Anchored
to the Leaves

Autumn by the *Sea*

my heart scaled an autumn cliff—
grasping for grace through the fog
when a copper light glowed from above,
but what i thought was a lighthouse
turned out to be *fall*

leaves on fire a hundred feet above the surf,
and i couldn't tell which would haunt me most
—their burning, or inevitable sinking

Autumn
by the Sea

kelp-like greens tried staying afloat amongst
the raging red seas in the forest—
but the full autumn tide overtook
all that was left of summer

maybe all the golden leaves
that once were green have
imposter syndrome, too

Autumn by the Sea

i know, a gilded world
is so heavy to hold

where do i fit
when the box
remains the same
but i do not

Autumn
by the Sea

earth traced the lines of change—
my world is so delicate right now, she sighed

do the leaves ever think
about when they will fall?
do they anticipate this
moment with broken souls?

Autumn by the Sea

i know i should let go, the leaf quivered,
but no one will tell me what happens next

when the time comes
you won't have to walk alone,
the wind reassured

Autumn
by the *Sea*

i dropped the burdens from my shoulders and whispered,
i cannot carry these anymore—

i think i understand, autumn replied

when morning came,
the white flags were reluctantly raised
to surrender all that was carried

one by one the burdens fell into the sea
like sunken treasures never to be found

Autumn by the Sea

the waves all disorderly ordered
lull my soul into this season ever-carefully
just before i drown

burning crowns tumbled to the ground
as if stolen in tyranny
and i marveled at their royalty—
wondering how their kingdom
ended in such devastation

Autumn *by the* *Sea*

is grace as golden
as i had once perceived?

i see you now, the trees whispered
i did not know how letting you go
would make you shine

Autumn
by the Sea

i mourned the leaves
tossed about by tawny waves—
an unanchored fleet of burning sails
that i could not save

promises echo off the water—

    i will find you again come spring, the trees cry

Autumn
by the *Sea*

i just want to be
a soft place to land,
                    earth said

i fall under the same minor melancholies,
sorting through truth and fiction
the same way october does with leaves

Autumn by the Sea

autumn by the sea is different
depending on what day you find it—
perhaps my heart is made the same

I WONDER WHEN AUTUMN

WILL TAKE OFF HER MASK

Autumn _by the_ _Sea_

the ineffable missing of someone
before they are gone leaves me grasping
for every bit of life around me

DEARESTFOLK POETRY

EVERY LEAF SEEMS TO HOLD
THE ANSWERS AUTUMN STOLE

Autumn
by the
Sea

earth held the leaf against her chest and cried—
all i ever wanted was a love that could change my life

what a vulnerable thing to be a tree—
both scaling clouds and buried grounds
and watching everything you gave,
                              leave

Autumn *by the* Sea

autumn towed her line
through the trees until their
matchstick frames faded
into a gull-grey sea

i frantically collect the leaves
like lost brittle shells
who always get overlooked

Autumn
by the Sea

look at this mess i have made, autumn cried,
—and i cried with her

what a beautiful
shakespearean tragedy,
watching earth die
ever-gracefully

Autumn
by the *Sea*

i turned the eroding leaf over in my palm
feeling like it gave so much—
and nothing at all

because the trees could not keep their seasons,
they released the end like rusted pieces,
and i, too, must leave for new beginnings

Autumn *by the* *Sea*

will you stay with me after the last leaf falls?

i think i've said goodbye too many times before,
i thought, running through the trees looking for spring—
knowing deep down you can only grow by dying

SEC. 3

*My Coastal
Ghost Town*

Autumn
by the *Sea*

i finally found my way through the trees
and back to my heart

—how long did i wander?

driftwood boarded the windows,
the lighthouse long extinguished,
and the cobblestones shuddered
beneath my feet as if they felt
how heavy a hollow heart
weighs upon their stones

Autumn
by the **Sea**

DID MY DESERTED STREETS

LEAD YOU TO A DIFFERENT TOWN?

grief passed through
the hometown of my heart—
homesick for loneliness

Autumn
by the Sea

the air was permeated with autumn gloom
—i could almost *taste* the grey

i grasped for the past
but all that remained
was a ghostly smoke—
slowly disappearing like
it had never known light

Autumn *by the* *Sea*

grief hung over me like harbor signs
all pointing to heartache

i leave lanterns around my crumbling walls
hoping someone might *save me* this time—
    because even a lighthouse needs refueled

Autumn
by the Sea

i stood in the courtyard
where the last leaf fell in utter silence—
so quiet, no one noticed but a tree

the breeze handpicked a leaf
and then failed to keep her

Autumn *by the* *Sea*

arrowed stems spin—
tiny broken compasses
forever asking
where do we go now—

—*where is the reef*
that protects the trees
from autumn?

Autumn
by the *Sea*

perhaps the trees and the sand
are more alike than i thought

it was all too much for the trees to endure—
so, i sighed, *is this what you really wanted?*

Autumn
by the Sea

everyone took advice from the leaves—
but me

all i can do is wait for the tides
to claim the ashes of the past

Autumn
by the
Sea

sometimes my heart lays quiet waiting
for something like your hand to dig me out

october exchanged garnets for coal
—she must be searching for diamonds

Autumn *by the* *Sea*

i wiped the soot from my heart—
i didn't know it would end like this,
i cried,
but i am still breathing

84

SEC. 4

Octaber Tears
Sink the Ocean

Autumn by the Sea

i could have sunk forever,
october recalled

i lived for the days
when an overcast sky
looked as if it might
burst into tears
at any given moment

Autumn *by the* *Sea*

do raindrops fall
the same way as leaves?

my soul is stirred about like a van gogh sky
—life does that sometimes

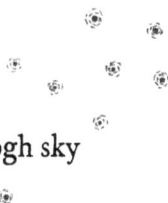

Autumn *by the* *Sea*

when my heart was a buried storm
october took my deepest shades
and brought them to the sea

though unassuming, she falls in the most
exquisite shades of sadness

Autumn
by the *Sea*

and the raindrops danced upon the ocean—
feeling both so small, but so vast

i cannot stop the storms in my soul,

the rain sighed,

but i promise to fall for you like no one else can

Autumn
by the Sea

there is something so comforting
when the sky spontaneously cries
that makes my tears feel right at home

—and the rain fell, and i could not tell
if i was breaking or healing

Autumn
by the **Sea**

*october seems to gather
more tears than the ocean*

my soft heart yearns for rain in all forms—
falling from both candle and sky,
smudged out scenes as mist meets sea,
yes — my heart longs to be flooded

Autumn
by the *Sea*

cloud-swept skies
are raining diamonds
that cut me to the bone

october rain haunts the sea
with its fallen voyage

Autumn
by the Sea

AUTUMN EYES SWIRL IN PALETTES

BLURRED WITH REGRET

the rain abandoned a familiar world
    just to show me how to let go

Autumn by the Sea

autumn is a library of skies
that picks suede-soft rain
to cover my story

the rain weeps over the leaves
like they are tattered pages torn from an old book

Autumn *by the* *Sea*

i suppose the rain fell in empathy for the trees—
or maybe because she foresaw
what the remaining leaves must endure

i offer roses to the sea as tribute
for the storm she endured

Autumn by the *Sea*

my ship moves upon waves
galvanized by october haze—
but grace is the captain
who once navigated similar seas

if i sink in the rain
will the ocean save me?

Autumn *by the* *Sea*

the waves lapped against my edges
and the rain softened my lines
as if salvaging the best parts of my heart

when the storm drained its rotting colors into the sea
my eyes didn't cling to the underworld beneath the ship
—they kept focused on the horizon

Autumn
by the *Sea*

—and so the raindrops cast
my reflection along the boardwalk—
thank you, i cried, *all i wanted was to be seen*

SEC. 5

The Boardwalk
Between Pendulums

Autumn *by the* *Sea*

this season advises me to let go—
but it feels so safe to hold on

i think my heart is like the hourglass—
it steadily tries to empty,
but always carries the same weight

Autumn by the Sea

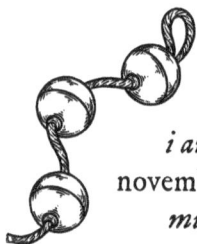

i am neither autumn nor winter,
november explained, *i am in-between—*
much like a heart balancing grief

my heart feels like the tide
—coming and going, yet always
remaining in the same place

Autumn by the *Sea*

i am unconsciously mystified by time—
some days i count each grain like sand,
but today time has disappeared
like a forgotten foggy morning

i walk somewhere
between
the sunlight of knowing
who i am
and
the shadows of questioning
who i will become

Autumn
by the Sea

SOME DAYS, I AM THE ROOTS——

BUT OTHERS, I AM THE LEAVES

i let autumn hold my despairs
because i could not seem to let them go

Autumn *by the* Sea

how do the trees face reinvention every season?

riptides continue to interrupt my healing
just before i reach the shore

Autumn by the Sea

will the sand only be remembered for losing things?

i am a ladder suspended
between heaven and earth—
climbing upon truth,
then falling down fears—
yet, rising again by morning

Autumn
by the Sea

i pace in my heart where the trees sway
like pendulums dipping from faith to fear

my tears feel too old to care
—but my heart still runs
through the feelings
like they have never met

Autumn
by the Sea

autumn's footsteps echo
gently along the weathered timber—
waiting for me to follow their path
that leads to letting go

SEC. 6

Dusting Fear
at Low Tide

Autumn
by the
Sea

my miseries sailed upon seas
that finally came home to a quiet harbor

it is nice to know i exist,
i whisper to the creaking floorboards

Autumn *by the* Sea

the shutters gently sigh against the cottage,
not quite ready to flutter away—
but slowly testing the strength of their wings

wild roses bloom in greige
as if drinking in the sea—
she is sick with storm
and i begin peeling away
her chipped petals
until i find spring

Autumn
by the Sea

i gently ask the dust, *what's it like getting older*—
but they cover their secrets from me

a stubborn sea mist clings to my window
their little scales veil my ocean view
and as i scrub over each briny spot
i find restoration in my heart, too

Autumn by the Sea

i watch the tides hit the shoreline—
inexact in its timing,
but all nonetheless meeting land

DEARESTFOLK POETRY

PERHAPS DUST IS MADE OF OCTOBER

Autumn by the *Sea*

i filed away my misfortunes in a cabinet of drawers,
slowly building a library for the fallen

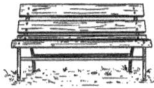

the why of things settles like dust
upon my empty bench of patience

Autumn
by the *Sea*

in my autumn state of mind
i am waiting to be found

i sit on the floor of my ceiling
and let my hair dangle to the kitchen tile below—
i don't come here often enough, i say aloud,
it feels nice to have a change of perspective

Autumn by the Sea

—and in my quiet sacred days
i was simply learning to be

i keep my regrets in the corner—
and like a haunting, they reach for my mind
every act of irrationality balances so delicately
and as i climb their recurring edges,
i peer down and call, to you—
please don't ever become a collection of my broken things

Autumn *by the* *Sea*

autumn relentlessly
turns over concepts
just like the ocean

you struck a match in my heart,
and though the walls are dimly-lit—
i am beginning to recognize myself again

Autumn
by the
Sea

i opened the window and called out to the trees—

perhaps i'm ready to let go, too

DEARESTFOLK POETRY

MY RESERVATIONS WERE MADE TO WALK THE PLANK

AND FIND REFUGE UNDER THE BRINY DEEP

Autumn
by the *Sea*

there was a layer in my soul that november winds uncovered,
and whether or not i was ready, it was time to encounter
the pieces autumn had left behind

it's time to let others in, i said as i swept away
the dust around the outskirts of my heart

Autumn by the Sea

the old clock chimes at dawn
once the sea retreats from the coastline—
it's a reassuring echo throughout the cottage
that awakens my heart to safety

peace has always been a tide—
return to me

Autumn *by the* *Sea*

i place a string of pearls around my neck and never
forget the beauty of grain-small beginnings

my fears retreat in low tide blues
and like an ocean my heart has grown garden green—
perhaps strength *is* mustered from fathoms below

Autumn by the Sea

i make windchimes out of my anchor
to ground my soul during stormy days

after searching through the day's ashes
i found myself reflected in diamonds

Autumn *by the* *Sea*

maritime tales line
my bookshelf like ships
who never forget
the seas they've seen

i found new horizons
beside the ivory curtains—
the ones in fishbone patterns
that towered next to my window
that overlooked a lighthouse

Autumn
by the Sea

i had left my heart out there somewhere—
perhaps long ago, but the beginnings of the shore
gave me hope in lost things restored

SEC. 7

The Amberlight Glows Across Tomorrow

Autumn *by the* Sea

i held the key in my palm and cried—
is this really all it takes?

i felt like a washed up shell
spinning through waves
as i climbed the lighthouse stairs
that pulled me into a twist—
but i could not stop now,
because the amberlight glows
across tomorrow

Autumn by the Sea

maybe in the end it will all become part
of something bigger than i can imagine

I BORROW THE HOPE OF LEAVES,
BELIEVING I, TOO, CAN CHANGE

Autumn
by the
Sea

the quietest strength lives
in the holding tight and in the letting go

i unbraid my feelings
and let them drop into your palms,
here—this is everything, i say

Autumn
by the Sea

the lighthouse lantern spilled over the inlet—
a patchwork of fallen light that the sea
harvested for every lost sailor

i released the ashes
of all i carried
and watched their wings
fly above the ocean—

farewell

farewell

 *farewell*

Autumn by the Sea

grief perched its quiet wings beside my heart and i gazed—

i know you now, and i am not afraid

peace had returned as quietly as she had left the room
you came back for me, i cried

Autumn by the Sea

—and next time,
i promise to never lose myself again

autumn threw its edges into the sea
and let the currents smooth it over
until all that remained was seaglass

Autumn *by the* *Sea*

i stepped into myself today
and now i will carve my name into
these old worn shoes that brought me here

i am finally standing on the balcony
looking down upon all the seasons i climbed

Autumn *by the* *Sea*

—and now that i am here,
i am simply spellbound
by the gentleness of the unexpected

—even after seeing the cracks
in my floorboards, you stayed

Autumn
by the *Sea*

THE LIGHT COVERED MY FLAWS

WITH A CLOAK OF FORGIVENESS

on the days you feel small,
let the seashells show you how to be found

Autumn
by the Sea

i am woven with the heritage of leaves,
knowing one day i will grow again

things fell apart for a time—
but i knew they'd come back together

Autumn *by the* *Sea*

like earth, i turn in patterns,
knowing my seasons are only mortal

so often life gives us a forest of ordinary things
that we must walk through
until it all becomes unbearably beautiful

Autumn ^{by the} *Sea*

i believe we were given autumn to know
that even as one thing ends,
we can always walk away gracefully

dearest autumn,
take my words as you quietly let go,
because i cannot help but think
we both tore out the same page

Autumn by the *Sea*

would i pay the price to fall again
if i knew, in the end, autumn poetry
would eulogize my agony?

AUTUMN SEEMS TO KNOW

WHAT WAS GAINED

WITH HOW MUCH SHE GAVE

Autumn by the Sea

maybe the trees are no longer haunted
by autumn because winter offered her peace

take the perspective of the sea
when you navigate autumn

Autumn _{by the} *Sea*

on my heavy days i look to the sea
—where a beautiful life exists below
despite being buried by waves

life is an ocean—
mending and breaking
giving and taking
yet, we come to the shore
again and again
with hopeful hands
and anxious feet—
never really knowing
what mood the tide will be

Autumn
by the
Sea

fill your soul with sand and sea
so that you might shift effortlessly
in the reckless storms of life

i will be in autumn—
you will be in the sea,
but we will both find release

Autumn by the Sea

of all the fragile things you hold—
don't forget about your heart

did life sever you, too?

i whispered to the branches,

if only they could see our roots

Autumn
by the Sea

tell me what you see from
your view in the lighthouse
and promise to keep the light burning

we must train our souls to feel—
because there will be days when
the answer arrives without a voice

Autumn
by the Sea

sometimes the sea spins things
so unrecognizably in order
to uncover hidden treasures

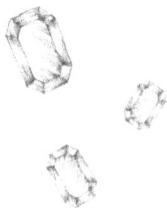

i often find myself
comforting november
because now i know
the language of fog

Autumn
by the Sea

the sea turns autumn into folklore

i once lived like the sea—
lowering the sails when there was no breeze,
but faith lives with open wings even in stillness

Autumn
by the Sea

the sea has roots
connected to the moon
that help pull her apart
from things she no longer needs

i knew autumn would return one day,
but that didn't stop my heart from building new castles

Autumn
by the Sea

yet, *despite it all*—
it ended more beautifully than it began

ACKNOWLEDGEMENTS

To Brett who fills my heart with a love beyond sea and sky—you keep me steady in the waves, I love you so much.

To Luella, Avett, Sanders, and Cohen for making my dreams of motherhood come true. Life would be empty without you.

To Lindsey, Hannah, and Kelly who inspire me creatively every day and are my constant sounding boards.

To Ryan who is a lighthouse in our family— never stop shining. You are a beacon.

To Mom and Dad who took me to the sea and showed me that faith is the greatest hidden treasure we can find.

To my readers who encourage me to keep writing—thank you for believing in my words.

To Jesus who has found me over and over and over again.

Ashley Archibald is the author and creator behind
Dearestfolk Poetry.

Her poems are inspired by
faith,
fairy tales,
folklore,
vintage finds,
and nature.

Ashley writes amongst the bluebonnets
and willow trees in Texas.

This is her debut poetry collection.

Instagram: @dearestfolkpoetry
Email: hello@dearestfolkpoetry.com

sending you the softest seas

YOURS EVERLY—

Dearestfolk
POETRY

www.ingramcontent.com/pod-product-compliance
Lightning Source LLC
Chambersburg PA
CBHW021617270326
41931CB00008B/747